20 HABITS TO BE A SUPERWOMAN

---◈---

SIMPLE 5-MINUTE HABITS THAT GIVE YOU ENDLESS ENERGY, PRODUCTIVITY, AND MAKE YOU AN UNSTOPPABLE BADASS!

BY **KATIE STONE**

Contents

Introduction

Hey there, I'm Katie!

In this book, you will learn 20 habits that successful and powerful women use to set themselves up for success and live a happier, more fulfilled life. These habits don't *guarantee* success, of course, but make it a lot easier to achieve whatever you aim for.

Since I know that your life is busy enough as it is, each chapter has one habit, so you can read them in short bites, and includes an action plan. These action plans help you adopt a habit and implement it in your life within 5-10 minutes.

In the first section, you will learn about habits that improve your health and well-being since you need a strong foundation for success. You will learn how to stay relaxed in a busy world, how to be happy every day, the simple magic that will make others do their best to help you succeed, and even how you can massively tip the scales in your favor by helping others.

In the second section, you will find habits that sharpen your mind and get you laser-focused on your goals. If you are feeling unmotivated or lazy, or struggle with doubt or insecurities – this is the section that will change your life. You will learn how to focus your energy to make every day productive, how to start believing in yourself, how to stop doubting your abilities, and how to become unstoppable on your road to success.

In the third and final section, you will find habits that improve your focus and productivity. While everyone else is running in a hamster wheel, working all day without making progress, you will escape this nightmare and start taking huge strides toward your goals instead. You will learn how to clarify your life and simplify decisions, how to plan your days, weeks, and years to put yourself on the path to success, how to keep an endless supply of motivation, and how to finally get all the things you still haven't gotten yet. Finally, you will learn the one difference that sets apart the best from the mediocre.

It doesn't matter what your goals are – from graduating to getting the promotion with the corner office to building a billion-dollar empire: You need a strong foundation and the mental power of a billionaire to achieve any of these things with ease. Read this book carefully, and you will have all the tools that you need.

Love,
Katie

Section I: Health & Well-being

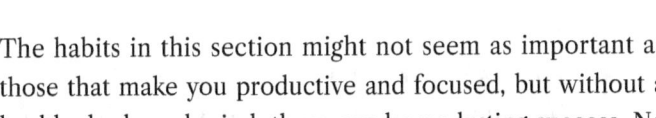

The habits in this section might not seem as important as those that make you productive and focused, but without a healthy body and mind, there can be no lasting success. No success is worth it if you are sick and depressed. In the end, isn't happiness part of your goal?

If you want to be successful in life, you cannot be unhappy and unhealthy every day. Working all day is possible, but if you can't enjoy it, you will burn out and break down eventually. Even if you do enjoy it, there's only so much your body can take. But this body is all you have, so treat it well – only then will it carry you to success and further so you can live your life on your terms.

Even if you don't have big goals – these habits will help you live a healthier, happier life, so read them carefully.

Waking Up Consistently
Habit 1

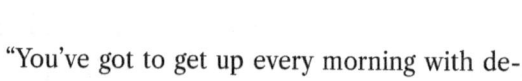

> "You've got to get up every morning with determination if you're going to go to bed with satisfaction." - George Lorimer

Waking up consistently (and earlier), especially if combined with a morning ritual, can drastically improve your life. Not just your productivity but your overall well-being and happiness, too! And if you have sleep problems, even those might get better.

Our bodies rely on schedules. The sun rises every day at (about) the same time, which used to be an anchor for our internal clock. But if you get up at different times every day and sleep in often, you mess up your circadian rhythm.

Don't worry – I'm not saying you have to go from getting up at 10 am to getting up at 5 am, run for an hour, meditate, do yoga, drink 10 liters of water, and work for six hours before breakfast at 7 am.

If you have to get up at a certain time every day to go to work, that's good. But do you really, or is the snooze button your best friend in the morning? Because guess what, that little button is the devil. If you can barely drag yourself out of bed every morning, start by setting a time a little earlier than necessary. If you *have* to get up at 7:40 or you'll be late, set the alarm to 7:30 and disable the snooze button.

It's hard at first, I know. In the beginning, I used to lie there and wonder if it was all worth it. You have to push through that and get up. After a week or two, you'll notice that it becomes easier, over time, even natural.

If you also go to bed at about the same time every day, your sleep quality will improve because of this consistency, so you won't even be as tired anymore. Make sure to sleep 8 hours every night whenever possible, and you'll be full of energy and focus every morning.

Over time, you can even begin waking up a bit earlier to get something done in the morning. I found that I'm actually more focused and productive now that I get up earlier than I used to. I love the feeling of having worked for an hour and finishing my workout by the time I usually got up. Overall, I certainly get more work done and sleep better every day. But dragging myself out of bed and into the shower is still hard.

You know the feeling when you don't have any energy the whole day? I had this quite often. Getting up earlier has actually *improved* this, too. When possible, I used to sleep and stay in bed until I felt well-rested. I usually was tired again in the early afternoon. Now, I get up even if I feel tired, but once I'm fully awake, I feel full of energy until the evening.

If possible, apply a consistent sleep schedule on weekends, too. Not necessarily at the same time, but get up without sleeping in or snoozing the alarm for three hours. Set your alarm to whatever time you need, but get up at that time.

The important thing is staying consistent, with a clear rule when you get up. That helps your body anchor its *circadian rhythm*. Basically, our bodies follow a rhythm that affects everything from how we feel, to our metabolism, and even our hormones. Getting up at consistent times improves our body's ability to function by anchoring it in such a rhythm instead of working against it. It also helps your mind be focused and sharp. Starting the day with an act of succeeding over your desire to sleep in. Start the day proving to yourself and the world that you are stronger than that.

Your Action Plan

To start building this habit, you need to find a time that you can get up at every day. Don't attempt getting up at 7:00 if you've been sleeping in until noon every day – start small. Pick a time and stick to it. *Every* weekday, you get up at this time. Partied late the day before? Tough luck, girl, get up!

This will help you build consistency and discipline and anchor you to your routine. Once it becomes a habit, you can start getting up earlier.

Additionally, going to sleep at about the same time every day makes it easier to get consistent sleep. If you get up at 7:00 every morning, going to bed between 11:00 pm and 12:00 am makes it a lot easier to get up than going to bed between 10:00 pm and 3:00 am!

Drinking Water
Habit 2

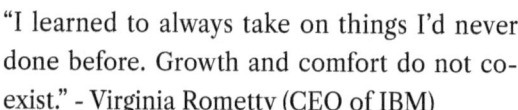

"I learned to always take on things I'd never done before. Growth and comfort do not co-exist." - Virginia Rometty (CEO of IBM)

Staying hydrated is incredibly important to maintain your body's performance and energy. Drinking lots of water and cutting sodas will keep you healthy and focused, improve your memory, and protect you against fatigue and headaches.

When you wake up, you haven't had anything to drink for hours, so a big glass of water is exactly what you need in the morning. Especially if you drink coffee, you must have a glass of water first, as coffee doesn't help with hydration.

In a study of young women, fluid loss of 1.36% after exercise impaired both mood and concentration and increased the frequency of headaches. 1.36%, depending on your weight, is about 1.5 to 2 pounds on average. That's only about four glasses of water.

As you probably know, you should drink between 8 and 12 glasses of water at least daily. So if you only drink a single glass of water between getting up and late morning, don't be surprised if you get tired, unfocused, unmotivated, or even headaches by noon!

Additionally, drinking water improves your metabolism and fills your stomach – so if you want to lose weight or prevent overeating, water is your new best friend! In a study, people who drank two glasses of water before meals lost 44% more weight over a period of 12 weeks.

This seems like a very mundane and even boring habit – but that's just life. Drinking in its entirety may seem pretty redundant, that is, until you stop doing it and die. Drinking lots of water might not make you feel that different today, but you'll notice the improvement over time.

Your Action Plan

If you still drink mostly sodas, consider slowly drinking more water or tea and less soda. If you try to switch to *only* water overnight, you'll get cravings for sweet drinks, making it hard to follow through. Instead, drink water in the mornings and throughout the day as much as you can and want to, eliminating sweeter drinks from your diet slowly.

Additionally, set rules for yourself. Drink water right after getting out of bed. Use an app to remind you to drink water throughout the day to stay hydrated. Ensure you drink at least 8-12 glasses (at about 8 ounces each) daily.

Staying well hydrated by drinking water makes you more capable and focused for all the challenges life throws at you and keeps you healthy and fit.

Getting Enough Sleep
Habit 3

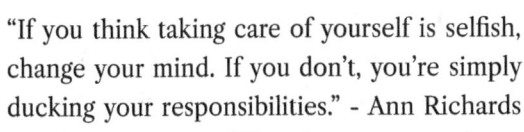

"If you think taking care of yourself is selfish, change your mind. If you don't, you're simply ducking your responsibilities." - Ann Richards (Former Governor of Texas)

If you've expected a chapter on "sleep only a few hours a night and get up at 5:00 am", I'll have to disappoint you. If you want to be successful in the long term, you need to take sleep seriously. Like drinking water, you might not feel the effects immediately, but you will.

We often hear that successful people have crazy schedules, waking up at 5:00 a.m., working out or going for a run, and starting the day in the office before others even get up. They get so much work done because they only sleep 4 hours per day and can work for 16 hours or more. But is that healthy?

It's true: the less you sleep, the more time you have to work. Getting up early and starting the day strong is a very effective method to be productive and focused the whole day.

But unless you want to eventually collapse from exhaustion and wake up in a puddle of your own blood like Arianna Huffington (co-founder of the Huffington Post) once did, you need to respect and value your sleeping time as much as your waking time. She made some drastic changes in her life regarding her sleep, and her success did not magically stop because she started to take care of herself.

Studies have shown that getting enough sleep daily improves your hormone balance, decreases stress, strengthens your immune system, and even improves your learning ability. They also found that sleeping uninterrupted is more beneficial than sleeping longer but with interruptions. If there is anything that often wakes you at night – do your best to get rid of such interruptions.

If you have implemented habit 1 and consistently get up at the same time every day, you can easily plan the right time to go to bed. Aim for 7-8 hours of sleep every night. But don't stop there. You may have the *quantity* of sleep, but do you have the *quality*?

While a lot of "normal" people fall into bed when they are tired, highly successful people often have rituals for sleeping, even using the night to prime themselves for success. After her breakdown, Arianna Huffington turned her bedroom into a sleeping palace devoted to resting well. Blackout curtains to keep the room dark (which improves the quality of sleep), no electronic devices (= no interruptions and no bright screens), and she always takes a hot bath before going to bed to calm down, relax, and put the stress of the day behind her.

Similarly, meditating for a few minutes before bed can help you relax and clear your mind to keep your sleep relaxing and restorative. If you have never meditated before, you can start by sitting down in a relaxed position (no need for cliché poses) and clearing your mind. Focus on your breathing. If a thought appears, let it float past you, and don't hang on to it. After a few minutes, you should be relaxed enough to fall asleep faster and have a calmer sleep. This is also great in the mornings to start every day relaxed, focused, and happier.

Your Action Plan

Create a simple schedule for sleep. If you get up every day at 8:00 am, set a reminder or an alarm to end the day at 11:00 pm or midnight, getting ready for bed.

Improve your sleep by turning off all electronic devices so you aren't interrupted by messages or notifications (or block all notifications if you use your phone for your alarm).

Don't look at any digital screen for an hour before bed to improve melatonin production (the hormone you need to sleep well – it is only produced when it's dark!).

Shower, take a bath, meditate, or do any other kind of ritual to get you ready for sleep every day so your body can prepare for the night and relax. This ritual will help you fall asleep faster and sleep better if you can leave your worries of the day behind instead of bringing them to bed.

Smiling
Habit 4

—◇—

"Spread love everywhere you go. Let no one ever come to you without leaving happier." - Mother Teresa

A genuine smile has so many benefits that it's hard to list them all. Before I even get to the benefits in your professional and personal life, I want to start with what's most important: Smiling makes you happy.

Even the act of smiling – whether you have something to smile about or not – makes your brain release dopamine, endorphins, and serotonin, the hormones that make you happy. It can also lower your heart rate and decrease blood pressure. All of that by simply smiling.

Additionally, if someone smiles at you, your orbitofrontal cortex is activated, which is responsible for feeling good and rewarded. We also tend to mimic the emotions of those around us, especially those looking directly at us. So, if someone smiles at you and you automatically smile back, it's like an espresso shot of good mood for the brain.

By smiling, you make yourself feel good and put your body in a positive state, but at the same time, make others feel good, too. Not only does that improve all kinds of personal relations (relationships, friendships, professional relationships, even interactions with strangers), but it also makes you more interesting and attractive, both for dating-related topics and for a professional impression.

People who (genuinely) smile a lot are usually considered more friendly and open but also more intelligent, confident, and successful.

Smiling whenever you can is a great habit to pick up that will become completely natural to you. Not only will it make you happier, but it will also directly improve your interaction with other people and how much those people like, trust, respect, and value you.

Of course, only smiling is not quite enough. That friendliness should be backed up by how you talk to people and interact with people. Simply greeting people with a warm smile when they walk into the room or talking positively instead of negatively reinforces that friendly impression. If you spread positivity with both your smile and behavior, you will be the lighthouse of happiness in other people's lives, and doors of opportunity will open for you wherever you go.

Your Action Plan

Start small: Whenever you feel stressed out or sad, find a quiet place where you can smile for 30 seconds. You might feel like an idiot, so find a place where no one sees you.

Then, start smiling intentionally whenever something nice happens – even something as simple as walking outside on a beautiful day. Pay attention to nice things and smile.

Then, begin smiling more at other people – whenever you greet someone, for example. Make it a habit to smile and laugh, and you will spread good mood wherever you go.

Helping Others
Habit 5

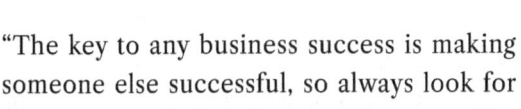

> "The key to any business success is making someone else successful, so always look for ways you can help other people succeed." - Patrick McGovern (Founder and Businessman)

Personally, I'm a big believer in Karma – or simply, "you reap what you sow." You could say, "The universe rewards you for being nice," but I'd rather be practical instead of spiritual and say, "The more you help others, the more others will help you."

In most interpersonal relationships, especially with people you don't know well or in business, it's simple: If someone asks something of you, they have to give something in return. That can be an "I help you, you help me" kind of deal, or simply an exchange of money vs goods. It's professional.

But once you start giving without asking for anything in return, even if it's just a small gesture, it becomes much more than that. People will see you differently, treat you differently, and go out of their way to repay the favor.

Being good to others also inspires them to be better themselves. If you freely help someone who's cheap and careful with money, you will be surprised by how generous they might become toward you.

And not only will people return the favor, but it also puts you in a very different position. Some people only work for their own gain. Other people also help others succeed. Which one would you offer a job? Invite to a private event? Invite for lunch? Once you start helping the people around you succeed, doors will start opening, and opportunities will be abundant.

Because if someone is always trying to get more of everything for themselves, we protect what we have so it doesn't get taken. But if someone gives freely of their own, we can also be generous with them, as we can trust that they are not out to exploit us. This goes for all kinds of resources: time, money, trust, and even smiles. (And you still remember how important these are?)

And it gets even better: If you help someone selflessly, others will notice. Even though you didn't help *them*, they still saw that you've been a good person and will be happy to help you as well – because you deserve it. Because we all want good people in our lives.

So, in short, do good and help others without thinking of yourself, and it will come back to you tenfold.

One more thing: Be mindful of people who will try to exploit your selflessness. There will always be those who will continue to take without ever giving. Immediately stop giving to those who will drain your energy, as they will prevent you from helping others who need and deserve your help more. Dare to say "no." – you will only be stronger for it.

Your Action Plan

Think of something nice someone did for you and thank them for it. A handwritten note or card would be even better. Or, do something nice for them in return.

Think of one specific thing you could do to help someone today. Help them, or at least offer your help.

From now on, when you go through life, be mindful of situations where you can help others – even if it's a simple gesture like holding the door for someone. In both life and business, always devote a part of your energy to helping others. The more you help others, the more you will receive in return.

Summary Health & Well-being

Your physical health and your mental health are strongly connected – you need both if you want to live a balanced, happy life. These five habits can all help you take care of your body and improve your general well-being and happiness. The habits in the next section will help you sharpen your mind, but without a healthy body and balanced life, it will be much harder to keep your focus. So, let's wrap up the first five habits again:

Habit #1: Waking up consistently

By waking up at the same time every day, you help your body anchor itself to its natural rhythm. This will help to keep you focused and stable when everything around you becomes stressful and chaotic.

Habit #2: Drinking Water

Drinking lots of water instead of sweetened drinks will keep your body hydrated, which has numerous benefits for your health and helps you power through the day. It lowers the risk of headaches and even improves your memory.

Habit #3: Getting enough sleep

Getting by on very little sleep has drastic consequences for your health. Sleeping the full 8 hours every day will not only provide you with enough energy for every day but also lower stress, improve your immune system, and improve your ability to learn new things.

Habit #4: Smiling

Smiling, even without reason, tricks your brain into actually being happier. Spreading this happiness by smiling around others will improve other's perception of you and make you appear more successful, more trustworthy, and even more attractive. Friendly smiles will open opportunities for you wherever you go.

Habit #5: Helping Others

Apart from making you feel good about doing something nice for someone, helping others also improves your social standing, earns you respect, and drastically improves your interpersonal relations, which will help you in all areas of life. Also, the people you help will do everything they can to repay the favor somehow – even if it's not immediately apparent.

Section II: Mental Power

———⬦———

Talk to successful people, and they will all tell you the importance of the right mindset. You see it in their eyes, in their body, in their every move – the people on top of the world think differently than most.

The habits in this section will help you remodel your mind, rewire your brain, and thus improve your mental power. This might all sound a little woo-woo, but it will all be clear soon. Think of your mind as a group of workers. If you put them in a messy room, give them no clear instructions, and just let them do it, nothing great will come out of it. However, give them a factory and the right tools, and organize them into a team, and they will be able to produce anything you want them to.

This process of "cleaning up" your mind and environment, refocusing your mental energy, and removing the blocks that hold you back will greatly improve your capacity to focus on the things that matter most.

Meditating
Habit 6

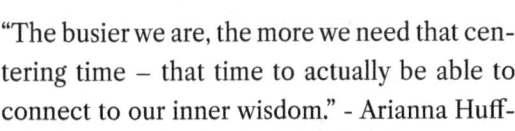

"The busier we are, the more we need that cen-
tering time – that time to actually be able to
connect to our inner wisdom." - Arianna Huffington (Co-Founder Huffington Post)

Many famous, successful women swear by meditation for
many reasons. It can help you start your day with energy and
focus, relax during difficult times, improve many aspects of
your life, and simply make you happy.

If you think of doing weird things with your mind in weird
positions – try to forget all that and start with an open mind.
Especially if you are just getting started, meditation and mindfulness should help you find peace and quiet in a busy world,
reconnect with yourself, and help you stay grounded. If your
life is hard right now, it can help you come back stronger, deal
with difficult emotions, or even find a new purpose in life.

Both mindfulness and meditation can be incorporated into
your life rather easily, even if you are busy. Start the day with

a short, 5-minute meditation session instead of checking your phone. Put your worries of yesterday away and calm down. Just sit somewhere relaxed and let your mind wander, but don't get pulled too much into thoughts. If you find yourself worrying, think about all the good things in your life instead. Do this for just five minutes every morning, and you will notice the difference very soon.

You can later expand this with concentration meditation, where you focus on a single thing, like your breathing, for some time, letting all other thoughts drift past you. This can help you improve your focus and bring clarity for the entire day.

You can practice mindfulness all day and get better at it the more you practice. Mindfulness is about being *aware* of your thoughts instead of blindly acting on them. If you get angry or nervous about something, step back and observe your emotions first. Where do these emotions come from, what upsets you?

Over time, you will learn to understand yourself better, be less at the mercy of your emotions (without suppressing them), and generally be more balanced and harmonious. In short, you will be much tougher emotionally and less upset by the insignificant rocks that life throws you. That gives you more mental capacity for what truly matters.

Your Action Plan

Find five minutes every day, especially when you are stressed out, and sit down to relax. Take a few deep breaths, calm down, and let go of all your worries for five minutes. You can continue worrying later if you must, but take a short break from all of it. Just breathe and think of the good things to come or happy memories of this week. Once you can do that with ease, you can look into more "advanced" forms of meditation. (Don't worry – it's all not that complicated.)

Also, whenever you react to something with a lot of emotion, try to take a deep breath and think about it for a second. Is that response justified? Especially negative emotions like anger, fear, or anxiety are often unjustified. Understand that you are not the slave of how you feel and that you can *choose* to be happy and positive, whatever happens. Don't ignore your emotions; accept that you feel them and that they are valid, but also choose not to act on them or feel bad for days because you don't have to.

Reciting Affirmations
Habit 7

———————◇———————

"Life is not easy for any of us. But what of
that? We must have perseverance and, above
all, confidence in ourselves. We must believe
we are gifted for something and that this thing
must be attained." - Marie Curie (Physicist)

Positive self-affirmations are scientifically proven to have
many benefits. They can rewire your brain to be more positive, perform better, and even improve your physical health.

All kinds of messages bombard our subconscious every day.
From TV advertisements to things our colleagues and friends
say, all these messages become beliefs in some way. Most of
all, the things we tell ourselves. I'll be honest here for a second
– I always talked myself down when I made a mistake. "Oh,
I'm so stupid," "I'll never get this done in time," "This will never
work",...

But those are dangerous thoughts. We say them, eventually
truly believe them, and then they become reality.

Instead, repeating positive affirmations to yourself daily makes you believe the best in you instead of the worst. It can help you be grateful for all you have, happy about where you are in life, and optimistic about your future. Just writing them down once can help you restore your confidence in yourself and remind you of what's important. Reciting them daily keeps you on the right path and strengthens you enough to overcome all kinds of challenges.

A good affirmation is in the present – something you can do or be right now. It's something you can believe in. Something tangible – "I am going to be rich" is bad for all reasons: It's not in the present (which means it doesn't help you in the present), it's not something you can actively do or be (so you can't act accordingly) and it's not very specific.

Instead, try something like "I am working towards my goals every day, and I know I will reach them in time." This is in the present (I am working every day), it's something you can do (not give up and be lazy, but keep working on your dreams), and it's a specific guide to what you are doing. It also gives you hope when you start doubting that everything will work out. Sometimes, the faith in ourselves to keep going is all we need.

The goal of an affirmation is usually to either remind yourself of your good qualities and potential, remind yourself to enjoy life, or keep you on track to get where you want to go.

Here are some examples for both categories:

- I speak with confidence and assurance
- I feel energetic and full of life

- I appreciate every moment throughout the day

- I feel wonderful and alive

- I am in control of my behavior and my actions

- I organize my priorities

- I make the most of new opportunities

- I am successful in whatever I do

- I am courageous and stand up for myself

- I am indestructible.

Your Action Plan

Write down one or two positive affirmations on a sheet of paper. Recite them a few times every morning, evening, or during your commute. You can also write one done to recite in the face of stress and pressure to keep you calm and sane. You will soon start to truly believe in your affirmation and feel its effect in your daily life.

Being Positive
Habit 8

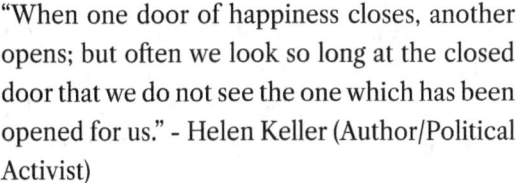

"When one door of happiness closes, another opens; but often we look so long at the closed door that we do not see the one which has been opened for us." - Helen Keller (Author/Political Activist)

The effects of thinking positively are similar to those of positive affirmations – they change how your brain thinks. You can quite literally change your world simply by changing the way you see it.

If you are in a negative state of mind – fear, anxiety, stress – your brain is in survival mode and only tries to get you out of this situation. Since we tend to feel these emotions a lot when we are under pressure from school, university, work, or even at home – we spend an awful lot of time being negative and just trying to escape.

But if you choose to be positive instead and manage to get out of survival mode, you suddenly have the capacity to see so many good things in your life, opportunities open, and you have time for happiness.

You might think that you need a holiday for that to happen – to get away from all the stress first. But that's exactly your survival mode talking. Remember the habit of meditation? You can create five minutes of positivity without going on a holiday. Throughout the day, you can make small decisions to be positive instead of negative, thus, piece by piece, changing everything.

And it's not just you who's affected: Once you start being more happy and positive in your life, people around you notice, too. We like to be around happy, relaxed people because we would like to feel the same. It gives you a magnetic pull, not just drawing in people but also opportunities. Challenges become less difficult and easier to overcome, and the rocks that life throws at you become nothing more than a nuisance.

This is not just a motivational speech – it's science. There have been countless studies proving that people who are optimistic and positive or get shown positive emotions are happier, healthier, live longer, and are more successful. Thinking positively improves your professional life, personal life, friendships, and relationships and will even improve the lives of the people around you.

Your Action Plan

If you want to create positivity in your life, there are a few ways to do that:

1) Meditate for a few minutes daily, thinking only about positive things in the present and near past or future.

2) Practice gratitude: every morning or evening, write down at least three things you are happy or grateful for on this day. By writing about positive experiences, you keep the negative ones from taking over and anchor yourself to happiness.

3) Take time to enjoy life, no matter what. Even if you are totally stressed out, take the time to spend with your loved ones, or treat yourself to something nice like a hot bath and relax. Unwind, relax, and remember that life can be good, no matter what else is going on.

4) Be mindful of your language: negative language such as "I can't," "impossible," and "unlucky,"... reinforce a negative perspective.

Change "I can't" to "It is difficult, but I believe I can," don't simply say something is "impossible" but "not possible with the tools I have." The more you tell yourself you can't do something, the less you can do it. Instead, tell yourself you *can* do it. And if you really can't, specify the *why*.

Eliminating Toxic Influence
Habit 9

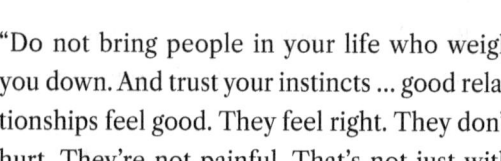

"Do not bring people in your life who weigh you down. And trust your instincts ... good relationships feel good. They feel right. They don't hurt. They're not painful. That's not just with somebody you want to marry, but it's with the friends that you choose. It's with the people you surround yourselves with." - Michelle Obama (Former First Lady)

Even if you start thinking positively – your life won't *really* change if you are held back by your environment. Most of us are surrounded by toxic influences that harm our striving to better ourselves. Cutting these influences out of our lives is one of the greatest steps you can take. But it can also be one of the hardest.

Let's say you're trying to lose weight and eat healthily. Then there's one of two friends on your side – either one who eats mostly junk food and wants to get you to eat takeout with him/her, or a friend who fully supports you and wants to cook healthy food with you together. Which one would you rather have at your side? If you stick with the first, you will have a very hard time reaching your goals; with the second, it's going to be not only easier but also a lot more fun.

We all have some people in our lives who, in some way, hinder us from becoming the best version of ourselves. They hold us back for all kinds of reasons, intentional or unintentional. Out of jealousy, spite, or simply by being who we don't want to be anymore.

If you have someone in your life who really holds you back, even if they don't seem to mean ill – be careful. Talk to them about it, that you are really trying to do "x" and that they make that harder for you when they are doing "y". And if someone keeps being in your way – it might be better to avoid that person. Someone who's truly a friend or means well would not stand between you and your goals.

If avoiding is not possible, like with colleagues at work, you might want to try addressing the issue very directly. If you are anything like me, you would worry about hurting people's feelings when confronting someone like that. Remember that they are not only hurting your feelings but are also making your life worse and diminishing your potential. Stand up for yourself and value your own life and goals over hurting someone's feelings a little.

The difference between being in an environment where the people around you support you and an environment where the people around you hold you back is immense. It's like running downhill versus running through knee-high mud.

Remember, not everybody has to like you – if you want to become the best version of yourself, you have to *be* yourself first, and that includes standing up for yourself.

Your Action Plan

Sit down and think about what you are trying to achieve. What are you struggling with, and is there anyone responsible for some of these struggles?

Go through life and pay attention: Who's supporting you, cheering you up, and talking you down, trying to stop you from achieving your goals?

Once you have identified these influences, you can choose to avoid them, or at the very least, be mindful of when they try to pull you down and resist firmly.

A Morning Ritual
Habit 10

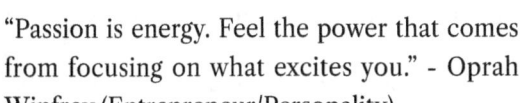

"Passion is energy. Feel the power that comes from focusing on what excites you." - Oprah Winfrey (Entrepreneur/Personality)

Just like pilots run routines before every flight, a morning ritual can help you ensure your day goes smoothly, without too much turbulence (or crash landings), and gets you to where you want to be.

Many successful women have a morning ritual, but it looks different for everyone—after all, every person is unique.

For example, Arianna Huffington said that a big part of her morning ritual is not looking at her smartphone or checking emails, but instead practicing yoga and meditation for a bit and setting her intentions for the day. Many other successful women in business get some physical exercise in every morning, a few minutes of yoga, 30 minutes of workout or even an hour of tennis.

Another important aspect of every morning for many is spending uninterrupted time with their partner and kids – even if it's just breakfast together. Starting the day off by being happy and with the people who mean the most to you makes every morning a good one, so you can start your day with positivity.

What's important is that you don't ignore the *ritual* part – it's not just something you usually do but a strict rule. Waking up at the same time every day and starting the day off with the right routine helps you anchor your mind and body, gives you focus and clarity, and makes difficult times easier to master.

These rituals are what you can hold on to when life gets hard, and they are what pushes you forward when life is going well. Especially when work seems to overwhelm you, knowing that every morning is you-time with your loved ones, your happy place, will be your rock to hold on to.

Apart from waking up at the same time every day, here are a few ideas that you can incorporate into your routine:

A refreshing shower and taking care of your skin & hair: Start every day looking and feeling your best by taking the time to take care of yourself first.

A good, healthy breakfast: Instead of something quick and unhealthy (or nothing at all), find something you look forward to every morning that gives you the energy you need for a powerful day.

A few minutes of meditation: Center yourself, leave your worries behind, and gather your focus for the day with a short meditation session.

Practice gratitude: Write down what you are grateful for every morning, ideally in some form of diary. If you practice consciously seeing everything that's good in your life, you will find it easy to be happy every day.

Set your intentions for the day: Think about the one thing or up to three major things you want to complete today. Focus on tackling these tasks first so you don't get overwhelmed by all the little stuff that doesn't matter.

Visualize your goals and your future: Whatever you are trying to achieve, remind yourself of it daily. Really think about what your future will look like so you never lose sight of it. This will help keep you on the path to achieving these goals.

Do some light exercise: Yoga, running, or even a short work-out – wake your body up and feel energized the whole day.

Your Action Plan

Write down a morning routine and follow it every day. It might take a while to get used to it, but if you stick with it consistently for 30 days, it will become natural and effortless. Don't start big – start with 2-3 habits every morning, taking up no more than a few minutes. Over time, experiment expand your routines based on what works for you. Slow and steady change is better here than overwhelming change all at once!

If you haven't read my book *Morning Rituals* yet, get it on Amazon for more ideas for powerful morning routines that make you feel your best every day.

Avoiding Self-Doubt
Habit 11

———————◇———————

"I do not try to dance better than anyone else. I only try to dance better than myself." - Arianna Huffington (Co-Founder Huffington Post)

Doubting your own abilities or your appearance is a major problem for many people, especially women in business. No matter how far you come or how successful you are – it won't banish that self-doubt. It will always eat away at you until you find ways to defeat it.

One of the biggest reasons for self-doubt is the comparison to others. You look at other successful people and think that they know so much more than you, have achieved so much more, or simply have such good charisma. You think you can't compete with them.

But in reality, they probably feel just as insecure as you, no matter how many millions or billions they made. They just learned to put up a confident front and ignore their self-doubt. And ultimately, even if someone is more confident and more capable than you – it's not a competition. They have their strengths; you have yours.

If you find yourself constantly criticizing yourself for not being good enough, or not knowing enough – ask yourself this: What do others actually expect of you?

Often, we pressure ourselves to know everything or be the best at everything. But those are unhealthy expectations that we will always fall short of. No expert will ever be able to answer *any* question during a presentation. It may be expected that you know the stuff you talk about inside-out and know enough about the broader topic to answer basic questions, but it's perfectly fine not to know every answer to topics outside the scope of your presentation.

The best experts are usually experts in a very narrow field and might not know that much in other fields. Accepting that you don't have to know or be good at *everything* is the first step to accepting that you are good enough. Make sure you set reasonable expectations for yourself and do your best to be great at what you do, and everything else will slowly fall into place.

One other little change can also make a big difference to you: Don't focus on yourself but on your purpose. It doesn't matter if you hold a presentation in front of a board of directors or your class in school. Remind yourself that it's not about *you*, but about the presentation. Those people are not here to judge *you* but to learn about your business strategies, your chosen topic for class, or whatever else you are talking about.

The more you think about yourself and judge yourself, the more others will do so, too. If you focus on doing an excellent presentation and providing valuable insights backed by in-depth research, it won't matter that you accidentally put on two different socks in the morning.

And if you do run into people who only judge you instead of seeing your value – don't take it personally. Those who judge the most usually have the biggest insecurities and fears of being judged (which is why they put others down to feel better themselves). Their critique is more about themselves than you, so let it bounce off you.

One trap that many people fall into is linking their confidence and self-worth to their achievements. Imagine you are building a startup. If you can get to a million dollars in profit in your first year, you will feel like a huge success. And you totally will. But then, what will your next goals be? And what happens to your self-worth if you don't achieve it?

At some point, you might set the goal of 700 million dollars in profit for the coming year and feel like a total loser because you only managed 650 million. That might sound ridiculous, but it's a very real problem. Instead of attaching your self-worth to successes and achievements, think about who you *are* instead.

Doesn't that make much more sense? Because no matter how hard you fail, you persevere and get back up. That's something you can be proud of. If you focus on how you failed, you will only feel bad about yourself.

Your Action Plan

Think about and write down the things that you criticize about yourself. That can be anything from your expertise and knowledge to skin issues or your weight.

Then, think about how much others expect of you. If you just started working at a company, no one expects you to know everything – they only expect you to do your best. Are you doing your best? Good! And they don't care about your skin problems either – they want results. The same is true for your friends or dates – they like you for *you* and don't judge you for every little pimple.

Do your best, deliver great results, be a good friend, and focus on your *purpose*; everyone will see the best in you. Focus on your flaws instead, and that's all anyone will ever see. Think about that every time you judge yourself for anything.

Finally, remind yourself of all your good qualities and personal strengths. That's who you are – strong and beautiful. You won't always succeed because failing is a part of life. But that doesn't make *you* a failure! Whenever things go bad, and you start judging yourself for it – remind yourself of that.

Reading Books Daily
Habit 12

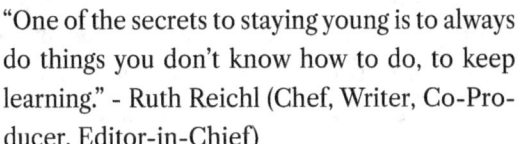

"One of the secrets to staying young is to always do things you don't know how to do, to keep learning." - Ruth Reichl (Chef, Writer, Co-Producer, Editor-in-Chief)

There's the old saying "Knowledge is Power" – and what else are books if not knowledge? Reading is one of the cornerstones of success for many of the most successful people in the world. You can read the very same books as them, understand how they think, and learn the same skills they've learned.

Warren Buffet, you know, the investor with a net worth of about $84 *billion*, said:

"That's how knowledge works. It builds up, like compound interest. All of you can do it, but I guarantee not many of you will do it."

He spends *hours* every day reading newspapers (the financial ones, not celebrity magazines) to stay on top of current events.

That's what gives him the edge to succeed, what has made him who he is today.

Bill Gates reads one book per week on public health, diseases, engineering, business, or science – not just on the topics he specializes in, but anything to broaden his knowledge and understanding. Mark Zuckerberg does the same, reading books with an emphasis on learning about different cultures, beliefs, histories, and technologies.

Whatever you want to achieve in life – building up a wealth of knowledge, experience, and skills will only help you get there faster and exceed your competition. Reading for just half an hour every day will quickly compound to having read many books that give you a significant advantage. In the age of eBooks, you can now read wherever you go and use those few minutes on the bus or waiting room to get some reading in. And maybe you watch one less episode of Netflix at night and read a good book to hone your skills or expand your horizons.

Your Action Plan

Dedicate a certain amount of time every day to reading (non-fiction) books. These can be books that teach specifically your profession, general self-development books, or even books on completely different topics that you find fascinating.

Instead of checking Social Media whenever you are bored on the bus, you could read a few pages on your phone (or eReader, or even a real book if you can bring it).

Stick to the habit of reading for at least a few minutes every day, and you will quickly build a wealth of knowledge using time that would be wasted otherwise.

Summary Mental Power

With the habits we talked about in this section, you can sharpen your mind and improve your life one small step at a time. Meditation, affirmations, and positivity all help you live a happier, more fulfilled life – because success is more than just money. Eliminating toxic influences and reducing your self-doubt helps you lose the weight that drags you down, while the morning ritual and reading pave your way for greatness. Let's go over these again very briefly.

Habit #6: Meditating

Meditation helps to ground you, brings you calmness and focus in a busy world, and improves your ability to focus and concentrate. Meditate for a few minutes every morning to start your day with focus and purpose.

Habit #7: Reciting Affirmations

Positive affirmations remind you of who you are and who you want to be, anchoring you in positivity even if the world around you seems harsh. They support you if you struggle with doubt or uncertainty and help you manifest your goals by firmly believing in them.

Habit #8: Being Positive

Being positive is not only good for your mental and physical health, it also makes things possible that seem impossible for others. Take some time every day to enjoy life and be grateful for all the good things you have. Avoid negative language and believe in yourself.

Habit #9: Eliminating Toxic Influence

Be mindful of people around you who drag you down with them or stand between you and your goals. Mention that they are hindering you and avoid them if they don't stop acting this way toward you. If necessary, don't be afraid to remove them from your life – your own success and happiness are more important than someone's negative attitude!

Habit #10: A Morning Ritual

Create a morning ritual for yourself to start every day with intent and full of energy. Gather your focus and prepare yourself for the day to come, so you can master any challenge life throws at you.

Habit #11: Avoiding Self-Doubt

Remind yourself that you don't have to be perfect or know everything. Focus on what value you can bring to the table and maximize your impact. If you focus on your strengths and what you offer, then that's what others will see. If you focus on your flaws or on avoiding those, that's all others will see.

Habit #12: Reading Books Daily

The knowledge and skills you learn from constantly reading books will set you apart from any competition you might have and give you the edge you need to succeed. Read for half an hour or more every day to become a true expert or broaden your horizons.

Section III: Focus

———————◇———————

In the previous section, you have learned to reorganize your mind to prime it for success. In this final section, you will learn eight habits to use that mental power with a laser-like focus instead of wasting it on "being busy" without getting anything done.

I also want to remind you that without implementing any of the habits in sections one and two, you will not be ready to fully enjoy the benefits of the habits in this section. After all, you can't build a house without a strong foundation, even if the foundation isn't always obvious.

These habits, especially the last two, can make a big difference in your life. If there's only one thing you learn from this book – make it the last two habits. Those will make the biggest difference with the least effort.

So pay close attention and read on – this is where the fun begins.

Having a Personal Mission
Habit 13

———⬦———

"Build something you're passionate about. As an entrepreneur, you have to have the passion and drive to stay the course." - Alexandra Chong (CEO and founder of Lulu)

It doesn't matter if you want to change the world with a startup or if you just want to get through the semester – a personal mission statement will help you reach your goals.

Think of it as a lighthouse – wherever you are, you never lose sight of it. With every step, you can move closer to it. It gives you an anchor in life, helps to keep you focused, and makes it easier to make decisions.

Your mission statement doesn't have to be permanent – you will revisit it regularly. If you are studying, your mission statement could be to graduate successfully with certain scores. Then, you'd have to change it, to reflect your next goals.

Also, it's only effective if you really keep it in your mind – writing it down and forgetting about it won't work. Put it up somewhere where you can see it daily, read it every morning, and remember it every time you go to bed. This mission statement will focus your energy and efforts so you can break through any obstacle until you reach your goals.

Such a statement should also serve as guidance. If your goal is to graduate with high scores, but you are often lazy and procrastinate a lot, keeping this goal in mind will help you make the right decisions. When you think about Netflix vs assignments, your mission statement will tell you clearly which of the two you need to pick. The only question is whether your mission is important enough for you to put it above most other things in life. (Hint: if it's not – it's not truly your mission. Dig deeper!)

Now, let's create your mission statement together. First, you need to define where you want to go. Graduating could be your goal, but I'd go a little further. Maybe you are studying medicine – but ultimately want to become a doctor and save lives. *That's* your mission. So, write down what you want to do, achieve, or be – for example: "I want to be a doctor and save lives."

Next, define the *how*: What will you do to reach this goal? "I will graduate by studying hard, watching less TV, and always doing all assignments on time."

If you have enough desire to reach your goal (become a doctor, save lives), you should be able to stick to your *how*. It will be hard, but your path is now clear. By sticking to that path, you know that every step you take is bringing you closer to your ultimate goal. And that's the power of mission statements.

This habit might seem a little redundant – you already know what you want anyway. But in the midst of the chaos that is our life, we often lose sight of our goals and focus too much on the wrong things. This habit can help you stay on track at all times.

Your Action Plan

Sit down for 10 minutes and write down your mission statements in two sentences: *what* you want to do/be/achieve, and *how* you want to achieve it. Then, put it up somewhere where you can see it daily, and make sure to read it out loud every morning.

From time to time, you might have to adjust it a little – do that! Adjusting the *how* makes sure you keep the path aimed directly at the goal.

Creating Action Plans
Habit 14

⸻◈⸻

"So often people are working hard at the wrong thing. Working on the right thing is probably more important than working hard." - Caterina Fake (Co-founder of Flickr and Hunch)

If you have completed the previous habit, you have your big goal and how to get there in mind. But if you don't want to get lost somewhere along the way, you will need to create regular action plans.

I'm sure you know that successful people use to-do lists in some way. But there is one big step between a long-term goal and a to-do list for the day. Using an action plan, you can map out weeks or months in advance and define the steps that lead you to your goals.

Let's take the previous example again: you are studying to become a doctor. Your daily to-do list would consist mostly of learning for whatever exam is around the corner and doing the assignments you were given. But if that's all you're doing, you will soon fall into a trot and probably lose motivation, as every day seems to be the same with no real progress.

Instead, you could make a list of all exams for this semester. Once you have passed all of these, you should be done with the semester. That's like a to-do list, but more long-term. This helps you keep track of your progress, so you actually feel and see that it's going well. Set yourself a goal for each exam, like the grade in this case, and note down the actual grade once you have it. This will help you break down the big goal of graduating into smaller goals. The two biggest benefits of that are first, it's a lot easier to focus on one exam at a time than focusing on everything at once, and two, you can celebrate a little and feel proud a lot more often with many small goals than with one big goal. Celebrating your successes is important!

But that wasn't the action plan just yet. After all, these were goals, not actions. Do you know the feeling of wanting to start learning in time for an exam, but then you end up starting too late once again? This tends to happen when you're busy with other things and don't feel ready to add even more workload by also learning for an upcoming exam before it's absolutely necessary. If you are already working at 100% just to keep up with the tasks for tomorrow, finding time to learn for the exam in two weeks might be hard. But if you plan ahead and reserve some time in those two weeks before an exam, it will be easier to balance the workload and focus on what's important.

To create an action plan, define the things you need to do, and allocate time for it. Most people tend to focus on smaller, short-term tasks first – pushing the longer tasks to the end of the to-do list. But then those smaller tasks keep piling on, and the big assignments or studying is neglected for lack of time. But successful people know how to prioritize, and all those small tasks are usually eating time without getting you results.

That's why you should take some time and figure out what is most important to complete your goals. For example, you could allocate two hours of learning every day in the two weeks before an exam. Schedule these learning sessions in advance and don't let anything keep you from them. That way, you make sure you start learning early enough and don't put it off because of other tasks. Additionally, you could plan three hours every Friday to work on that year-long project. We tend to push these off, too, since there's so much time left. Until the project nears the end, and we realize we f*cked up. Be smarter than that by planning half a year or a year in advance. This will make sure you stay on track by focusing on what's important instead of focusing on small things first and never getting to the important tasks.

Your Action Plan

Write down your sub-goals for this year (or semester if you are studying). Write down what you have to do to reach these goals, and how much time you will need for that. Make sure to plan for a little more since unforeseen delays are almost guaranteed.

Plan ahead for your most important tasks, which you want to complete daily, weekly, monthly, or on specific schedules.

These are your priority tasks, which you should always focus on and make time for.

Focusing on the important actions that bring you forward is the difference between running in circles and actually getting stuff done.

Planning Your Days in Advance
Habit 15

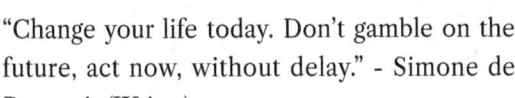

"Change your life today. Don't gamble on the future, act now, without delay." - Simone de Beauvoir (Writer)

Do your days ever feel like stumbling down the stairs, going too fast to stop, hoping you can somehow stay on your feet until you reach the end? You have so much stuff to do that you don't even know how you are supposed to finish it all. Planning your days in advance may be the answer you need.

If you look at successful people's calendars, you will often see that it is densely packed with all kinds of meetings, events, and plans. If you want some of their time, you might have to request it weeks in advance. But if someone comes to you with a request – do you tend to try and do it as soon as possible?

We can't always focus on what drives us forward the most. But if we take on every little task first, we'll never get to the important tasks. That's why it can be *very* beneficial to plan your day in the evening before. If possible, use the time in the morning for your most important tasks. Block that time out for anything else. You can get the small stuff done later. This way, you can make sure that you get the important things done, no matter what else piles up.

Remember, just because something else comes up today doesn't mean it's always more important. Prioritizing well is key. Since you now have a personal mission statement and an action plan, it should be a lot easier to figure out what tasks get you there the fastest. If a task doesn't help your goals at all, you need to think about whether it is *really* necessary for you to do it, or if there are other ways to get it done faster.

One habit that many executives have is not checking their emails constantly. They only do it once or twice a day. This way, they can fully focus on the task at hand, since new emails would only be distracting. As they have their day planned out anyway, if anyone needs something, it won't be today. Yes, this means they say "No" or "Not today" a lot. A habit you need to start doing if you don't want other people to write your schedule.

Think of it like detoxing – you flush as much crap out of your schedule as you can and try to prevent any new unimportant tasks from blocking your time.

Your Action Plan

Using a to-do list or similar system, sit down every evening to write down your most important tasks for the next day. Assign as much as possible of that from morning to noon when you have the most energy. Once you have completed the important tasks, you can spend the rest of the day with less impactful work.

You probably block out times for anything where you definitely can't work or do stuff – like a doctor's appointment. But are you doing it for yourself, too? Start blocking out the time you dedicate to working on things that are important to you and really bring you closer to your goals. That's sacred time that others don't get to touch – it's YOUR time!

Whenever new tasks come in – don't do them immediately. This will only distract you and destroy your focus. Schedule them for later today or, even better, another day. Before you do, put it in one of three categories: "Important for me," "Has to be done," or "Kinda should be done." That's the order in which you should schedule these tasks, too! Don't let unimportant tasks steal your time and dare to say no to them. Often, the consequence of not doing them is not that bad, and only short-term. What is the consequence of not doing the tasks that are important to you? You'll never reach your goals and dreams and will live an unfulfilling life. It should be easy to decide which of these to do first.

Making Time For Yourself
Habit 16

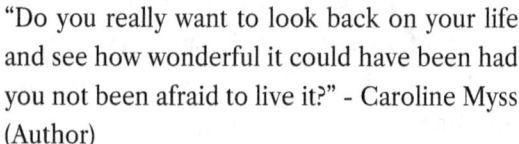

"Do you really want to look back on your life and see how wonderful it could have been had you not been afraid to live it?" - Caroline Myss (Author)

If you read about successful people, you often hear that they work harder than anyone else, sometimes even sleeping in the office like Elon Musk is doing during stressful times. While that may work for some, it certainly doesn't work for most. If you want to avoid burning out and breaking down, you have to learn to make time for yourself.

If you read about any successful personality, you will find one of two options: either they work crazy hours, are suffering from stress and all kinds of health-related issues, and their personal relationships and marriage suffer, too. Or, they manage their personal time very consciously, making an effort to spend time on themselves, their family, and their health.

The reason why there is rarely anything in between is simple: if you have a burning passion for your business like most super-successful founders have, you work on your dreams with all your time and energy. They usually don't spend afternoons in front of the TV or go out three times a week. That's why they are either complete workaholics or have to make an effort to reserve some time for themselves.

If you are thinking that you are not one of these people, that you are spending enough time for yourself and what's important to you – that's good. But there will be times when the workload is overwhelming, where you find yourself working all day. That can be cramming for an exam, finishing those reports for your boss, or working on your own business. Sometimes, life is stressful. And as the saying goes - *when it rains, it pours*. That's the time when people burn out and break down.

That is why it's important to always plan some time for yourself. Even just consciously spending every morning and treating yourself with a good breakfast could be enough to keep dangerous burnouts away. Being able to let go of all the stress will also increase your productivity overall, improve your life's balance, and give you the strength to overcome challenges that might otherwise break you.

If you are in a relationship, make sure to pay attention to it. It's usually one of the first things that suffers when we get stressed out. However, a healthy, happy relationship is exactly what you need when work seems to be killing you. Trying to find time in your schedule might be hard. And whatever you plan, something might come in between. Don't let it. Instead, create a time for you and your loved one that is untouchable. For example, the time between getting up and leaving for work – use that time and spend it together. You can be stressed out about work later, making breakfast together and catching up on each other's lives is just as important.

Another factor is the influence other people have on your time. If you feel like you're constantly busy and never seem to find time for yourself, the problem might be solved with a simple "no." I know I have struggled with this myself – someone asks me to do something, I say yes. Someone invites me to something, I say yes. Someone asks me if I have time, and I say yes. I used to drop everything if someone needed anything from me. But if you are always doing things for others, you won't have any time for yourself. This point ties in a lot with the previous habit of planning your day in advance.

In the end, no matter what you want to achieve in life, we all want to be happy. Maybe your goal is to only work five hours a week and get by. Or maybe you want to build a business and become a multi-millionaire by the age of twenty-five, working eighty hours a week. Either way, if you can't find time to enjoy your life, you won't succeed. Because even if you managed to reach that goal, if you're not happy, what's the point?

Taking time for yourself doesn't necessarily mean working less. It can mean that you take the time to work on the things you enjoy most. And usually, even if you do take the time off work to spend with your loved ones, the increased energy and happiness will boost your productivity enough to compensate for it easily.

Your Action Plan

If you are in a relationship, or getting into one, talk to your partner about how you can make sure to spend quality time together despite busy schedules. This can be as simple as having a regular breakfast or dinner together where you are not allowed to talk about work.

Think about the things you want to do in life besides work, such as spending time with friends, having hobbies, or maybe traveling. Set some time aside for these and put them in your schedule. Treat them as important as you would any meeting.

When someone asks you to do something, even fun pastime activity like parties, remind yourself that you are allowed to say no. If you would rather spend the evening alone at home, taking a hot bath and reading a book, feel free to say so. If you want to do what you love and be happy, you have to make that time deliberately – sometimes it's harder than it seems.

Celebrating Your Achievements
Habit 17

"Beware of monotony; it's the mother of all the deadly sins." - Edith Wharton (Author)

Celebrating your achievements is one of the best ways to keep your motivation up and stay on track with your plans. If you don't properly enjoy your successes, the work and struggles are all you're going to see – a recipe for burnout.

Think of a little kid or even a baby. How long can you get them to sit and listen, or sit and watch in silence? Not very long – attention span is not a strength of tiny humans. Now that we've grown up, we can work for years just so we get a title when we graduate, or until we get the promotion and a corner office. But are we really that much better?

The main difference between that little kid and a grown-up is that you have to be disciplined to keep working even if it gets boring and you don't feel like it. Because you understand what it means to think long term, a kid does not. However, it doesn't change the fact that just like the kid, we lose motivation and joy just the same.

The thought of finally getting everything we've worked so hard for is motivating, but that motivation fades if you work day in and day out without making progress. You might be able to keep working regardless, but you won't find joy in it anymore.

Being stuck in that hamster wheel can feel like hell. But you can escape it. Not in a few years, not when you finally retire. You can start tomorrow. It feels like a hamster wheel because nothing changes, and you are working without getting anywhere. Changing this can be as simple as changing how you look at it.

You achieve things all the time; they're just not as grand as the goals you aim for. But you can't ignore all those smaller victories, or you'll never stop being proud of what you've done.

Set yourself goals – every time you hit them, you succeeded at something. Even if it's as boring as "have all reports ready on Monday by 4 o'clock". If it's even a little bit challenging, completing it is a reason to celebrate a little. Maybe don't pop the champagne just yet, especially not in the office, but maybe treat yourself with a piece of chocolate, a good tea, or simply take a five-minute break. And then maybe set the goal a little bit higher for next time.

Searching for and creating personal victories in your everyday life is a great way to get out of that trot and feel like you're actually going somewhere. Because you are. You just didn't see the progress you're making. And if you don't feel like there is a point to anything, you might not give your best. Once you start seeing those little victories, you will want more. You put more effort in. You succeed even more. People notice, and that promotion is suddenly much closer than you thought. But most importantly, you have way more fun at work.

And if you think that something isn't worth celebrating – think again. If you were a salesperson landing a big client for your company, resulting in a nice paycheck for you – that's a reason to celebrate, right? Of course, only until you think about how other people make that much money every day and more. It's all relative, so don't play down your victories. Even something as simple as getting up in the morning without snoozing even once can be hard. But you still did it, so be proud of yourself and stop playing it down. You don't have to tell everybody at work that you managed to get up this morning (yeah, they would probably think you're crazy), but if you don't feel good about getting up on time, why even bother? However, if you *do* feel good about every day you get up on time, it will be much easier, and your brain will *want* to get up early instead of sleeping in.

By celebrating and acknowledging every little victory in your life, you can be more motivated and happy, build momentum, and train your brain to enjoy working again. It loves the feeling of validation and happiness when you succeed once again.

Your Action Plan

Sit down for five minutes and write down everything you have done well today. Do this every evening before you go to bed. Write down everything you did well, every victory, and everything you can be proud of.

Additionally, pay attention throughout the day to every one of these little victories. Look forward to them, achieve them, celebrate them. Really treat yourself with something, even if symbolic, for every bigger victory.

Finally, start setting goals for yourself, even for everyday tasks. Without goals, of course life feels like a trot: there are no achievements and no cause for celebration.

Taking Care of Your Home
Habit 18

———◇———

"If your home environment is good and peaceful and easy, your life is better and easier." - Lori Greiner (Entrepreneur, Inventor, Shark-Tank Investor)

There are numerous studies linking a clean, organized home to improved health, better sleep, and better focus. So if you have wanted to clean your place for a long time, but kept pushing it off – this chapter is for you.

Do you know the feeling of eating at a buffet, especially if you decide to try all the dessert options, and then you're so exhausted you can't move the rest of the day? Try replicating this feeling with a healthy salad – you won't be able to. The buffet is like a messy home – fine if enjoyed occasionally, but a problem if you have it daily.

Similar to eating too much, a messy home can overload your brain with too much input. As our brains always try to process our environment, lots of clutter will make it work way harder than a tidy apartment. If everything around you constantly reminds you of things you still have to do, your subconscious is constantly jumping from one thing to the next.

It is scientifically proven that people with tidy homes are more relaxed and happy, and less likely to be depressed or fatigued. So if you want to improve your life – cleaning up your home is one integral part of that.

Since this is a book about habits, how can you make a clean home a habit? Start by scheduling certain tasks weekly – like vacuuming, cleaning your bathroom, or tidying up your living room. Set a certain time aside every week for cleaning. If you stick to it, the difference will be remarkable.

First, you might need to declutter mercilessly. Hanging on to stuff you don't need is only holding you back. I won't go into details on decluttering here, but it will be necessary to start with that.

Once you have a decently tidy home and clean up weekly, you should start working on keeping it clean every day. Stop putting stuff just *anywhere*, put it where it belongs immediately. Don't leave stuff lying around but put it back as soon as you don't need it anymore. Make it a habit not to leave things around because each thing you leave around is a reminder of a task uncompleted (putting it away again). Each of these may only be a tiny bit of work, but subconsciously, they pile up to *"Oh my god, I still have to do so much."*

That's why constantly keeping a clean, tidy apartment helps you keep a focused, relaxed, and happy mind.

Your Action Plan

Schedule some time this week to declutter your home. Set aside at least two hours and put away all distractions for that time. Turn on some music and clean up.

Then, schedule at least one hour every week for cleaning your apartment again – vacuuming, cleaning your bathroom, kitchen, and bedroom... and putting things back where they belong.

Once your place looks tidy and clean, make it a habit to keep it that way every day – it actually saves you time! It will also improve your health and happiness and help you be more relaxed and energized.

Going After What You Want
Habit 19

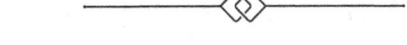

"Power's not given to you. You have to take it."
- Beyoncé Knowles Carter (Singer, Business-woman)

Is there something that you would like to have or get, but didn't get it yet? That can be something as simple as an invitation to a party or a date, but also a promotion at work. Now the important question: Have you directly asked for it yet?

Many people, especially shy, introverted people, enjoy working outside the spotlight of attention. And that's perfectly fine. However, without any attention on you, your work, your effort and even your achievements and results may be overlooked. So, when the time for a promotion comes, you might not be given as much thought as you deserve. Simply because unlike others, you are not constantly putting the attention on yourself.

But that doesn't mean that you have to change that. What you need to do, though, is accept that without being in the spotlight, things won't always come to you on their own. People will not go to you first, but to those in the spotlight. That means if you want something, you will have to go after it yourself.

"Ask and she shall receive! Women often find it hard to ask for things, whether it's a business opportunity or a salary raise. We simply expect others to recognize our value and hard work. Asking for what you want in a gracious, thoughtful way often results in getting what you want, so put your fears aside and ask for what you want. You might just get it!" - Alexandra Lebenthal *(President and CEO of Lebenthal & Company)*

This quote was too fitting to not include it here. If you want something, not asking for it is insane. It's like being hungry, sitting down in a restaurant without ordering, and hoping someone would still bring you food. That's not how it works.

Asking for something, whether it is a promotion, an invitation, or anything else, will give you a much bigger chance of getting it. Even if you only mention that you are interested – it is much more likely that that person will get back to you than if you didn't show your interest. (Because how else would they know you are even interested if you don't say it?)

If you are worried that it might be disrespectful, rude, or ego-istic to simply ask for everything you want, It's not. Unless you know you are going to hurt someone by asking, it's probably fine. People don't think badly of you if you start going after what you want – they will respect you for it and most likely even envy you for being that courageous.

Your Action Plan

Write down five things you currently want, now or in the near future. Then, for each of these, think about a way how you can ask for it or express your interest (not "show your interest subtly" – *express* it!).

Make it a habit to say what you want, even if it's really hard at first. The fact is, if you make a decision or help decide something, others are often *thankful* that they don't have to decide it themselves!

Taking Risks
Habit 20

———◇———

"Courage is not not being afraid, it's being afraid and doing it anyways." - Gina Bianchini (Entre-preneur)

One of the biggest differences between successful people and non-successful people is the ability to take risks and dare to try something new. Without this, you probably will never get far in anything.

It's a harsh reality, but if you aren't taking risks, you are staying safe in your comfort zone – where you will stay until you're old. Not a cheerful prospect. Staying safe might sound nice, but what if you could take risks and soar? If you ask any successful businesswoman, they will tell you that they are taking risks every day.

So what's their secret for not failing?

It's simple: they do. All the time. Expensive failures, even. And yet, despite all of them, they are now CEOs, executives, or world-leading athletes. Because they took calculated risks and failed a few times but also succeeded. And this sum of failures and successes is much greater than slow, steady progress without risk.

So in reality, it's either "succeed massively a few times and fail often" or "rarely fail but never really succeed" – what are you going to choose?

Of course, simply taking any risk you come across isn't the answer. You need a way to calculate the actual risk vs the possible reward in a decently objective way. Here's one system that could work for you:

First, assess the risk and rate it on a scale of 1-10: 1 being a very temporary, small setback, 10 being life-destroying. Be critical about it, though, and don't blow anything out of proportion. We tend to overrate risks, especially if they disrupt the status quo – but change is often better than you think.

Second, do the same for the positive outcome: 1-10, 1 being no tangible benefit, 10 being positively life-changing.

Then, estimate the likelihood of those options. This might be the first aha moment, where you realize that the risk is well worth the reward.

What's important to keep in mind is your ability to recover. Imagine you'd like to ask your boss for a raise. How bad would you rate the risk? I'd say anything higher than 2 is stupid in most cases. Even if your boss would say no, they would probably not think of it again – they've got bigger things on their mind. Of course, when you stand in front of them, the fear of being laughed at might overwhelm you and make it feel like a huge risk.

One of the worst fears you might have in your professional life is probably losing your job. However, is that really bad enough to not take any risks? Assuming you have some sort of savings, your worst-case scenario would probably be that you have to find a new job. Maybe you'd actually get one with higher pay, in a better company, or with nicer colleagues.

If you want to succeed at things – anything – then you need to reevaluate the risks you aren't taking. The more you attempt and risk, the more you will learn to believe in yourself. This confidence will help you grow beyond anything you now think you can do. That's the difference between people waiting for a promotion and people building billion-dollar businesses. (Although you certainly don't have to run your own business to succeed)

Your Action Plan

Write down at least five things you *could* do, but don't do because of the risks. This can be anything from going sky-diving to asking for a promotion or even telling that annoying colleague to turn the music on their headphones down. Write down and rate the worst-case scenario, the realistic bad-case scenario, the result if you succeeded, and then finally, the likelihood of each.

This should help you put things in perspective so you can dare more, take more risks, and start succeeding!

There's the saying of doing something every day that scares you. Make this mindset your habit and dare harmless-but-frightening things when you come across them. You will outgrow your old, scared self faster than you'd believe.

Summary Focus

———◇———

Once your body and mind are primed for success, you need the focus to pave the way for what you want to become and achieve. These habits will give you a focused determination that will push you through any obstacle you will face – and there will be many.

Habit #13: Having a personal mission

Have a personal mission statement – who do you want to be, what do you want to achieve, and how do you want to achieve it? Keep it in your sight and in your mind every day, so you won't let anything come between you and your goal.

Habit #14: Creating action plans

Focus on the tasks that drive you forward by planning your steps in advance, so you don't drown in meaningless everyday tasks. Write down the goals and sub-goals you want to achieve this year and what you have to do to reach them. These are your priority tasks.

Habit #15: Planning your days in advance

Prevent an overload of time-blocking nonsense by planning your days in advance as much as possible, blocking out time dedicated to the most important tasks that drive you forward.

Habit #16: Making time for yourself

No matter the workload, if you forget to take care of yourself, you will not be able to take the pressure for long. Make time to treat yourself and spend some time doing what you love or spend it with your favorite people. There's no excuse to neglect yourself.

Habit #17: Celebrating your achievements

Make boring days more fun by paying attention to all the little victories, and start celebrating them, even if only symbolically. Create fun little challenges for yourself and take pride in completing them. Make productivity fun again!

Habit #18: Taking care of your home

A messy home leads to a messy mind – unclutter your workplace and apartment to improve your focus, happiness, and energy. Keep it tidy by making it a habit to constantly organize it.

Habit #19: Going after what you want

Whatever it is you want, you are missing out if you don't ask for it. Learn to say what you want openly and with confidence, start making decisions for yourself, and you will become a natural leader who will get what she wants.

Habit #20: Taking risks

Leave your comfort zone to become the amazing and successful person you want to be. Learn to see risks as necessary and good and take them whenever the potential reward is worth it. Dare to attempt even the scary things, as those usually get you the farthest (and make the best stories).

Bonus Section: The Key to Successful Habits

If you've journeyed with me through the chapters of this book, you've already started shaping the habits that form the bedrock of success and well-being. You've learned about waking up with determination, embracing healthful routines, and empowering your mind with resilience and focus.

But there is a nuance to this that you need to keep in mind before you start implementing any or all of these habits.

While the typical overachiever might want to implement *all the habits*, that's not actually a good thing – and it might even make you *less successful*.

More important than anything is moving through life with *intention*.

I was absolutely guilty of "being busy" and following all kinds of great habits, while completely neglecting what I truly wanted out of life. You always need to start there and circle back frequently. Figure out the *destination* you're trying to reach rather than simply "moving forward."

This will not only provide tremendous clarity, but also make all progress feel smooth and effortless. It will eliminate many mental blocks and resistance from your journey.

Most importantly, it will make sure that you won't make "massive progress" and then one day realize that you hate the life you have built.

Let's get started.

Crafting Your Vision

Welcome to the first steps of intentionally crafting your future. The power of a vision isn't in the abstract—it's in the concrete. To make your aspirations tangible, you must be precise about what your life should look like in the near and distant future. Let's begin by setting clear, time-bound visions for 1, 5, and 10 years from now. These aren't merely goals; they are destinations on your personal journey through life.

Visualizing one year ahead

Start with just one year from now. Where do you want to be? What do you want to have achieved? Maybe you're looking to earn a promotion, finish a degree, or have finally taken that solo trip abroad. Picture the details—where are you living, what does your daily routine look like, who are you spending time with? Write these down in vivid detail. Remember, the more specific you are, the more real it will feel and become.

Two more things: First, you can be quite specific here, but you can and should leave things open as well. For example, you might say, "I have travelled to five different countries", but leave the specific countries open for future-you to decide.

Second, and this one is more important than you might realize: **Make sure to include feelings and emotions more than just facts.**

For example, you might want to say, "I am financially independent" or "I earn x amount every month" – but how does that *feel?* Because, in most cases, what you truly long for is not a certain number in your bank account but how it makes you feel.

Maybe it's the feeling of safety that you're after. Or maybe it's the ability to treat yourself to nice things without feeling guilty.

If you neglect the emotional side, you may end up reaching the "factual" goal without achieving the feeling you were after.

Dreaming five years forward

Five years allows for more significant changes. Perhaps you see yourself transitioning into a new career, starting a family, or living in a different country. Consider the skills and experiences you'd like to have by this point. Think about the relationships in your life and the state of your health. Envision where you stand in your community or your professional field. These are the middle chapters of your upcoming story, filled with growth and achievement.

As you might notice when attempting to write your five-year vision, a lot more can drastically change in five years. You could go from being single to having a child – or living in a different country with an entirely new life.

Even more so for this vision: Focus on what matters the most to you, the core of what would make your life feel fulfilling in five years.

Write everything that comes to mind, then cross out things you could do without and still be happy.

A decade into the future

Ten years gives you the canvas to paint a comprehensive picture of your life. It's long enough to transform any aspect of your life completely. Do you own your business? Are you an expert in your field? Have you written a book or perhaps changed the lives of others through philanthropy? Or have you moved to a farm and live off the land to escape the hustling & bustling of the modern world?

Reflect on the legacy you're building. What are your core achievements? How have your values and lifestyle evolved? The clarity you develop here sets the stage for every step you take from this point on.

This exercise can be quite challenging because it will push the boundaries of what you know about yourself.

You might find out what you care about above all other trifles – which may currently be in your focus. You might also find that you actually have no idea what your dream life looks like ten years from now.

While you may be tempted to skip over this and only think about it for a minute... don't. Take an hour of undistracted time and truly think about it.

I personally recommend taking a pen and paper rather than using your phone or computer to type. I find that going old-school allows our ability to think creatively to come out fully.

Once you are done, get ready for round two – and dive even deeper.

"It's all about you, girl"

With your visions clearly set for 1, 5, and 10 years, it's time to shift focus slightly. It's not just about what you'll achieve and the kind of life you live, but also who you need to be to reach these milestones. This is about aligning your identity with your aspirations and transforming internally and externally.

There are two important lenses to look through for this exercise: the person you have to be to *reach those goals* and the person you have to be to *live that life*.

For example, let's say your future self is in great physical shape. One trait this person might need is "consistency," especially in the face of resistance. If you give up easily, you'll never get into great shape!

But another way to look at it is the act of *being* in great shape. What does that take?

You may have found activities you love, such as team sports, windsurfing, climbing, Pilates, or strength training. You may have also started cooking healthy meals at home rather than ordering in often.

You will find that the second type of trait is usually more important, as a person who loves running is much more likely to run often than a person with discipline.

So, in other words: Who will you be that makes the life you want natural and effortless?

Write as much as possible about this person. Fill a whole page, and then keep going if you can! You need to get to know this person intimately – after all, it is you!

Aligning daily actions with your vision

The visions and the person you need to become are not distant dreams; they are templates for your daily living. Every choice and action should reflect your movement towards these endpoints.

Start by integrating small steps into your everyday routines that are in line with your future self. Align your morning routines, work ethic, learning habits, and social interactions with the person who lives in your visions.

I find that the easiest way to do this is to shift your consumption first. What kind of people do you follow on social media? What kind of videos do you watch? What kind of books do you read?

You tend to mimic the people you learn from and look up to, so find people that closely resemble the person you want to become.

Another important factor is your environment – if you want to be a successful business owner, but all your friends are happy to do the least possible professional work, you'll be held back. Find people to hang around with who are living the life you want for yourself!

It's also important to mention that crafting your vision is not a passive process; it's an active, ongoing practice that requires constant attention and dedication. Keep revisiting and refining your visions. Life changes, and so can your goals, but the clearer you are about where you want to go and who you want to be, the more likely you are to get there.

And remember, the path to these visions isn't linear. It's filled with learning and adapting. Each step, each revelation builds upon the last, bringing your envisioned future into the present. Let this chapter be the map that guides you from who you are today to who you will become tomorrow and beyond.

I have found that, like anything, life will be unexpected – but it will often work in your favor if you let it. Don't be upset if things don't move on the path you have imagined. You will have to balance a certain degree of control with the ability to go with the flow.

Daily Alignment with Future Goals

Creating a vision and understanding who you need to become to realize this vision are crucial steps. However, the real magic happens in how you live your daily life – how you align each day's actions with your long-term objectives.

It's like a boyfriend who ignores you all week, then brings you flowers once – it's not the gestures that define who you are, but who you are the rest of your time.

I believe it's also more important who you are when things are *bad*, when you are pushed to your limits, and when you are tempted to "cheat."

To revisit the example: It's easy to have one nice date or vacation and be present with your partner – but can you still make time for them when life gets messy? The end of the honeymoon phase is often when you're "back to reality" – and if things are breaking apart as soon as there are any bumps in the road, the relationship is bound to end soon. Your hopes, dreams, and future work the same way.

Habits make your future self

There is no need to be gloomy, though. Each day presents a new opportunity to shape your destiny. The actions you take today lay the groundwork for your future self. How you structure your day, the habits you cultivate, and your decisions should all be steps toward becoming who you want to be.

If you want to make consistent, long-term progress, it's best to focus on the things you repeat consistently, including daily and irregular habits.

The goals you set for the day, week, and month directly reflect who you will become. And if you don't set any – don't be surprised if you're not becoming the person you wanted to be.

In addition to setting goals in advance, you need some form of review as a consistent practice. Daily, weekly, and monthly reviews are all great for various levels of reflection. Without course corrections every now and then, you may notice far too late if you have gone off course.

These two habits are the only ones I consider essential, no matter who you want to be. Other habits are typically highly dependent on the person you want to become, the goals you want to achieve, and the life you want to live.

A professional athlete might want their diet dialed down to the exact macro- and micro-nutrients daily without deviation. On the other hand, a passionate travel blogger might want to be surprised every day with all kinds of new dishes, street food, and exotic meals. It's all about your personal dream life, not about "right" or "optimal"!

No matter the specifics, there are a few ways to make it easier to stick to your new habits more easily:

Start Small: Begin with manageable changes and gradually build on them. If you want to read more to expand your knowledge, start with a few pages each day and slowly increase the amount. It's better to start *tiny* than not to start at all. Especially if you are doing something "out of character" for you, let it become natural and habitual, no matter how trivial your habit might seem at first.

Make it easy: While a massive scene focuses on "doing the hard work" and "hustling," there is wisdom in doing the *easy work*. Because what is easy for you may be difficult for others – because it aligns with your true purpose, talents, or passions. Sometimes, all it takes is finding something you enjoy doing so much you don't even consider it work – then double down on that.

Be Consistent: Consistency is key in habit formation. Try to perform your new habits at the same time and in the same place every day. This consistency helps cement the behaviors into your daily routine.

However, don't get hung up on this and avoid becoming dependent. For example, morning coffee is more than a habit for many – without it, they can't function. Don't confuse habits with addictions! A habit is supposed to empower you but as an optional improvement. If you can't stay flexible and adapt, you become rigid rather than empowered.

Celebrate Small Wins: Recognize and celebrate the small victories along the way – because in reality, there are no "small" wins... just *wins*. Each day you adhere to your new habits, you move closer to your future self. Celebrating these small wins keeps your motivation high and reinforces positive behavior. The behavior – especially in the face of difficulty – is more important and celebration-worthy than the big success at the end.

This is a common trend among high-achievers: The "big win" often matters less to them than the journey and the *pursuit* of the win. That's how they stay driven at all times – they don't need motivation to keep going, the activity itself is what they enjoy.

So, how can you tap into this kind of power to make your own journey smoother, more enjoyable, and more fruitful?

Consistency over Intensity

In my experience, it's often not the progress that is the problem but the setbacks. Eating healthy is easy when there are only healthy foods around – but most people easily get thrown off-track once there's cake on the table, snacks in a bowl, or emotions best buried in a big bucket of ice cream.

It works the same with almost any goal: as long as you stay on track, it's actually very difficult to fail. Have you ever looked at it from this perspective? You'd be surprised how easy "difficult goals" become when you simply walk a clear path without deviation.

In the modern world, especially on social media, distractions are like the sirens of ancient myths – enticing and dangerous, capable of pulling us off course. The key to avoiding these distractions lies in recognizing what most frequently causes your attention to waver. Whether it's the allure of social media, the false urgency of endless emails, or even well-meaning friends and family who demand your time. Identifying these distractions allows you to build defenses against them, like massive walls and moats around a castle.

One effective strategy is setting clear boundaries around your time and attention. This might mean designating hours when you're unreachable, shutting off notifications to preserve periods of deep work, or educating those around you about your availability.

Prioritization is another critical skill. Distinguishing between what truly matters and what merely seems urgent can prevent you from wasting time on tasks that don't align with your long-term vision.

Personally, I have noticed that the biggest threat is often not the "big distraction" but a "small tweak." For example, if you are trying to lose weight, you might be lured by a new type of diet. You should do Keto! Three days later, you're trying a vegan diet instead. Then it's Mediterranean, back to low-carb, Paleo, and so forth.

It *feels* like you are still on track with your main goals, but the constant switching, changing, and chasing shiny new "shortcuts" often lead you in circles.

Despite what your brain (and influencers, ads, and friends) might try to tell you: It is okay to stay on your current path if you have done a good job of picking a valid strategy!

More often than not – like with dieting – all these options are perfectly viable ways to lose weight. You're not switching because your chosen path doesn't work, you're just switching because it *feels good*. The problem: It also means you avoid doing the work, and thus get trapped in a cycle of "improving."

Even with the best-laid plans, it can sometimes feel like you're making no progress at all. It's during these times that trusting the process is more important than anything. Building patience is crucial; change rarely happens overnight. Celebrate the small milestones along the way – each step forward is a victory and confirmation that you are moving in the right direction.

Read that last sentence again. *Each step forward* – regardless of the outcome. Sometimes, you have to try and fail a dozen times until you finally have the breakthrough you need. We tend to overestimate the results in the short term and become impatient, which is when many good plans are thrown overboard. Trust the process and stick with it – consistency is often more important than having the "best plan."

However, flexibility is equally important. If certain approaches or habits aren't bringing you closer to your vision, be willing to adapt your strategies. Change is constant, and your ability to pivot without losing sight of your goals can make or break your success.

The difficulty is knowing when to pivot and when to hold your course. One thing is rarely up for debate, though: pausing, stopping, or even giving up.

Consistency is perhaps the most critical element in the journey to your future self. It's not about achieving perfection each day; it's about persistent effort. Developing and strengthening daily routines that support your goals makes it easier to maintain this effort, even on days when motivation is low.

The best advice for consistent effort is to make it as easy as possible. Do not trust your willpower or discipline; they will fail you. At best, you can power through, but you will be drained of all energy and motivation in the process.

Use apps, tools, or whatever techniques work for you to make consistency easier and more enjoyable. Whether it's apps that track your habits or project management tools that tie your daily tasks to your broader objectives, these resources can provide a visual reminder of your progress and help keep you focused.

For example, listening to audiobooks or podcasts is my favorite way to make running more enjoyable. Otherwise, my head is filled with questions like "How much longer?" and "When am I finally done?"

Consistency also cultivates resilience. It reinforces your capacity to meet challenges head-on and continue moving forward. In the current age, resilience is in short supply. Simply becoming better at not being thrown off course will make you stand out far above most competitors in almost any field.

Finally, regular reflection on your progress and setbacks helps you to adjust your path as needed. Progress alone is not the goal; intentional and directional progress is. Sometimes, the biggest progress you will make is learning from mistakes and adjusting your course as necessary.

The easiest way forward

With all of that said, there is one fundamental truth that underlies all of these principles. If you take away nothing else, let it be this:

You only become more of yourself, closer to your truth, and more of what you believe in.

If you consistently struggle with becoming your goal self, maybe it's the goal – you can only become *yourself*; all attempts to become someone else will inevitably "fail."

You can't "make yourself care" about things you don't care about, nor should you. A good rule of thumb that I have learned to live by is to eliminate "shoulds" from your life as much as reasonable.

Don't do things because they are expected from you or because you think you're supposed to do them. Do them because YOU care about them – or don't do them at all.

Eliminating the wrong goals will also eliminate much of the resistance most people face. Think about it, how difficult is it for a child to play? How difficult is it for an artist to paint or draw?

If you want to become healthier, don't try to force a certain diet, but find a style of eating that feels best for you. Find ways to make it effortless. You don't get a medal for trying hard, but you get results if you can make it easy instead!

Which leads me to my last point: **What's "easy" is usually what you believe in the most**.

If you believe you were born to be a clumsy, awkward, but loveable artist – that will be your natural self. That's likely how you were raised and the identity that was reinforced consistently over the years.

It's *easy* because you have years of experience embodying this identity. But you can choose to embody a different identity at any time.

That's why the exercise at the beginning of this chapter is so important – it shows you who you will become in pursuing your dreams.

It's not about *creating* a new persona but about finding a different side of you, all the potential buried within you.

The best way to bring this person to life is simply to believe in them – in yourself. If you can have an unwavering belief that you will be this future version of yourself, there will be no obstacle too big and no distraction too tempting.

That's how massive goals become easy. How difficult trials become journeys.

How your dreams become your reality.

Next Steps

You are now at a crossroads. You can go on living life the way you did before, or you can take action and implement the changes as outlined in each of the chapters. I've intentionally written each of the action plans in a way that makes them easy to follow and not require too much work or change in your life. Adopting any one of these habits can literally start today. I've also included a summary of every habit at the end of the book. You can use this for a quick refresher in a week or two.

Here's how to <u>guarantee</u> you will succeed with your new habits: First, you need to start small – one or two habits. Write them down, including *what* you do daily, *when*, and for *how long*.

Second, you must stick to these new habits for at least 30 days. This is not only because results are rarely immediate but also because following these habits will become progressively easier. Think of it like learning a new language – you won't see any results after a week, but if you stick to it for a few months, you might already be able to lead very basic conversations.

The secret of successful habits is consistency: When you first start, the habit might not make a noticeable difference – but keep it up, and even a small habit can lead to massive changes.

There is one more "hack" if you want faster, easier, and more enjoyable results: Start your new habits with a friend or group of friends. You'll hold each other accountable, motivate, and inspire more progress.

Who do you know that deserves more success, energy, or happiness? Share this book with them and start your journey together!

Get at least two friends together to maximize your chance of following through and getting the results you're after.

Give and Receive

———◇———

I firmly believe that if you do good deeds and show kindness to the world, you will receive the same in return – often in unexpected ways, but always more than you gave.

These books are my contribution to making the world a better place, and there is a simple way for you to make an impact as well:

Please leave a short review and share your biggest learnings and breakthroughs with others so more readers will find this book.

The more people read these books, the more people I can help – and the bigger our impact on the world... together.

It only takes a few seconds, but these small acts of kindness and contribution will make not only the world but also your life a better place.

Taking only ten seconds to write a review could...

...help someone get their degree and dream career
...help someone raise healthier kids by being able to spend more time with them

...help someone improve their well-being and health by finally following healthy habits

...help someone create something amazing that will change the world

Many of the greatest inventors, businesspeople, and creators had defining moments in their path that set them up for success – often, it was a small act of kindness from someone else who had no idea how massive the impact of their small deed would be.

So please, take a few seconds and **leave a Review** for this book.

You can also scan this QR Code to be taken straight to the review page:

Thank you for making a difference – for me, for future readers, and for the world.

Love,
Katie

Read This Next

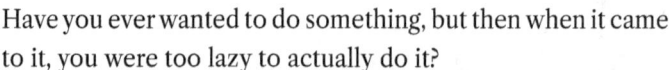

Have you ever wanted to do something, but then when it came to it, you were too lazy to actually do it?

Of course, we all struggle with it sometimes. First, we are full of energy, full of ambition. "No, but really – I will get up early tomorrow and clean my apartment, go work out, and then have a healthy lunch."

And then we ended up watching Netflix until late at night, sleeping in the next day, not doing anything we planned, and feeling bad about it. It happens to all of us.

But that doesn't mean that you will never get things done!

What you need is to understand why this is happening to you, and then use a simple system to get things done much easier. And once you are done, you can spend the rest of the evening watching Netflix without the guilt of doing nothing.

That's exactly what you will learn in this book. How to easily find motivation for anything, accomplish things you thought impossible, and then still have MORE time for all the fun things in life!

Order "Get It Done" now on Amazon!

All Habits Summary

Habit 1: Waking up consistently

By waking up at the same time every day, you help your body anchor itself to its natural rhythm. This will help to keep you focused and stable when everything around you becomes stressful and chaotic. A consistent sleep schedule improves your quality of sleep and your energy throughout the day, even if it is really hard to get up on some days.

Your Action Plan

To start building this habit, you need to find a time that you can get up at every day. Don't attempt getting up at 7:00 if you've been sleeping in until noon every day – start small. Pick a time and stick to it. *Every* weekday, you get up at this time.

Habit 2: Drinking Water

Drinking lots of water keeps your body hydrated, which has numerous health benefits and helps you power through the day. It lowers the risk of headaches and even improves your memory. Swap sweetened drinks for water whenever you can to reap the full benefits.

Your Action Plan

If you are still drinking mostly sodas, consider slowly drinking more water or tea. If you try to switch to *only* water overnight, you'll get cravings for soda, making it hard to follow through. Instead, drink water in the mornings and throughout the day as much as you can and want to, eliminating sweeter drinks from your diet one step at a time.

Habit 3: Getting enough sleep

Getting by on very little sleep has drastic consequences for your health. Sleeping the full 8 hours every day will not only provide you with enough energy for every day but also lower stress, improve your immune system, and improve your ability to learn new things.

Your Action Plan

Create a simple schedule for sleep. If you get up every day at 8:00 am, set a reminder or an alarm to end the day at 11:00 pm or midnight, getting ready for bed. Improve your sleep by turning off all electronic devices so you don't get interrupted by messages or notifications (or block all notifications if you need your phone for your alarm).

Habit 4: Smiling

Smiling, even without reason, tricks your brain into actually being happier. Spreading this happiness by smiling around others will improve other's perception of you and make you appear more successful, more trustworthy, and even more attractive. Friendly smiles will open opportunities for you wherever you go.

Your Action Plan

Start small: Whenever you don't feel so good, find a quiet place where you can just smile for 30 seconds. You might feel like an idiot, so find a place where no one sees you.

Then, start smiling intentionally whenever something nice happens – even something as simple as walking outside on a beautiful day. Pay attention to nice things and smile.

Then, begin smiling more at other people – whenever you greet someone, for example. Make it a habit to smile and laugh, and you will spread good mood wherever you go.

Habit 5: Helping others

Apart from making you feel good about doing something nice for someone, helping others also improves your social standing, earns you respect, and drastically improves your interpersonal relations, which will help you in all areas of life. Helping someone will also make that person and others want to do nice things for you, too – opening doors to many new opportunities.

Your Action Plan

Think of something nice someone did for you and thank them for it. A handwritten note or card would be even better. Or, do something nice for them in return (something they did not have to ask for). Think of one specific thing you could do to help someone today. Help them, or at least offer your help.

From now on, when you go through life, be mindful of situations where you can help others – even if it's a simple gesture like holding the door. In both life and business, always devote a part of your energy to helping others. The more you help others, the more others will help you in return.

Habit 6: Meditating

Meditation helps you ground yourself, brings calmness and focus in a busy world, and improves your ability to focus and concentrate. Meditate for a few minutes every morning to start your day with focus and purpose.

Your Action Plan

Find five minutes every day, especially when you are stressed out, and sit down to relax. Take a few deep breaths, calm down, and let go of all your worries for five minutes. You can continue worrying later if you must, but take a short break from all of it. Just breathe and think of good things to come or happy memories of this week.

Habit 7: Reciting Affirmations

Positive affirmations remind you of who you are and who you want to be, anchoring you in positivity even if the world around you seems harsh. They support you if you struggle with doubt or uncertainty and help you manifest your goals by firmly believing in them.

Your Action Plan

Write down one or two positive affirmations on a sheet of paper. Recite them a few times every morning, evening, or during your commute. Put as much belief in them as you can – find reasons those affirmations are true instead of doubting yourself.

Habit 8: Being Positive

Being positive is not only good for your mental and physical health, but it also makes things possible that seem impossible for others. Take some time every day to enjoy life and be grateful for all the good things you have. Avoid negative language and believe in yourself.

Your Action Plan

Meditate for a few minutes daily, thinking only about positive things in the present and near past or future. You can also practice gratitude: every morning or evening, write down five nice things that happened today that you are happy about. Also, take time to enjoy life, no matter what. Even if you are totally stressed out, take some time to spend with your loved ones, or simply treat yourself to something nice like a hot bath. Finally, be mindful of your language: negative language such as "I can't," "impossible," and so on reinforces a negative perspective on life.

Habit 9: Eliminating Toxic Influence

Be mindful of people around you who drag you down or stand between you and your goals. Mention that they are hindering you, and avoid them if they don't stop acting this way toward you. If necessary, don't be afraid to remove them from your life – your own success and happiness are more important than someone's negative attitude!

Your Action Plan

Sit down and think about what you are trying to achieve. What are you struggling with, and is there anyone responsible for some of these struggles?

Go through life and pay attention: Who's supporting you, cheering you up – and who's talking you down, trying to stop you from achieving your goals, not believing in you, and telling you so?

Once you have identified these influences, you can choose to avoid them, or at the very least, be mindful of when they try to pull you down and resist firmly.

Habit 10: A Morning Ritual

Create a morning ritual for yourself to start every day intent and full of energy. Gather your focus and prepare yourself for the day to come so you can master any challenge life throws at you. This will transform the daily trot into purposeful strides toward your goals and bring mindfulness and clarity into your life.

Your Action Plan

Write down and follow a morning routine for yourself every day. Include things like a refreshing shower, a healthy breakfast, a few minutes of meditation, some light exercise, practicing gratitude, setting your intentions and goals for the day, or visualizing your future.

Habit 11: Avoiding Self-Doubt

Remind yourself that you don't have to be perfect or know everything. Focus on what value you can bring to the table and maximize your impact. If you focus on your strengths and what you offer, then that's what others will see. If you focus on your flaws, or on hiding them, that's what others will see.

Your Action Plan

Think about and write down the things that you regularly criticize about yourself. These can range from your expertise and knowledge to skin problems or your weight.

Then, think about how much others really expect of you. We usually put way more pressure on being perfect than others do. Do your best, deliver great results, be a good friend, and focus on your *purpose*, and everyone will see the best in you. Focus on your flaws instead, and that's all anyone will ever see. Think about that every time you criticize yourself harshly for anything.

Habit 12: Reading Books Daily

The knowledge and skills you learn from constantly reading books will set you apart from any competition you might have and give you the edge you need to succeed. Read for at least a few minutes every day to become a true expert or broaden your horizons. If you can make the time, read for 30-60 minutes a day. The more you read and learn, the better you will become.

Your Action Plan

Dedicate a certain amount of time every day to reading (non-fiction) books. That can be books that teach specifically your profession, general self-development books, or even books on completely different topics that you find fascinating. Instead of checking Social Media whenever you are bored, read a few pages. As long as you keep reading, your expertise will be constantly growing.

Habit 13: Having a personal mission

Have a personal mission statement – who do you want to be, what do you want to achieve, and how do you want to achieve it? Keep it in your sight and in your mind every day so you will relentlessly get closer to this goal.

Your Action Plan

Sit down for 10 minutes and write down your mission statements in two sentences: *what* you want to do/be/achieve, and *how* you want to achieve it. Then, put it up somewhere where you can see it daily, and make sure to read it out loud every morning.

Habit 14: Creating Action Plans

Focus on the tasks that drive you forward by planning your steps in advance, so you don't drown in meaningless everyday tasks. Write down the goals and sub-goals you want to achieve in this year and what you have to do to reach them. These are your priority tasks.

Your Action Plan

Write down your sub-goals for this year (or semester if you are studying). Write down what you have to do to reach these goals, and how much time you will need for that. Make sure to plan for a little more since unforeseen delays are almost guaranteed.

Plan ahead for your most important tasks, which you want to complete daily, weekly, monthly, or on specific schedules. These are your priority tasks, which you should always focus on and make time for. Focusing on the important actions that push you forward is the difference between running in circles and actually making progress.

Habit 15: Planning your days in advance

Prevent an overload of time-blocking "keeping busy" tasks by planning your days in advance as much as possible, blocking out time dedicated to the most important tasks that drive you forward.

Your Action Plan

Using a to-do list or similar system, sit down every evening to write down your most important tasks for the next day. Assign as much as possible of that from morning to noon when you have the most energy. Once those tasks are out of the way, you can focus on less important tasks. Getting the less important tasks out of the way first is the wrong approach – you'll be exhausted and tired when you get to the actually important tasks.

Block out time dedicated to further your own goals and don't let anything interfere with that. Don't try to squeeze in every new task that pops up, or you'll never get the big challenges done.

Habit 16: Making time for yourself

No matter the workload, if you forget to take care of yourself, you will not be able to stand the pressure for long. Make time to treat yourself and spend some time doing what you love every day, or spend it with your favorite people. There's no excuse to neglect yourself.

Your Action Plan

Think about the things you want to do in life besides work. Things like spending time with friends and loved ones, hobbies, or maybe traveling. Set some time aside for these and put them in your schedule. Treat them as important as you would treat any meeting. Also, remember that you are allowed to say no to things you don't want to do – otherwise, others will control your schedule, and there won't be much time left for yourself.

Habit 17: Celebrating your achievements

Make monotonous work more fun by paying attention to all the little victories and starting to celebrate them, even if only symbolically. Create fun little challenges for yourself and take pride in completing them. Make productivity fun again!

Your Action Plan

Sit down for five minutes and write down everything you have done well today. Do this every evening before you go to bed.

Additionally, pay attention throughout the day to every one of these little victories. Look forward to them, achieve them, celebrate them. Treat yourself with something, even if symbolic, for every bigger victory.

Habit 18: Taking care of your home

A messy home leads to a messy mind – unclutter your workplace and apartment to improve your focus, happiness, and energy. Keep it tidy by making it a habit to constantly organize it.

Your Action Plan

Schedule some time this week to declutter your home. Set aside at least two hours and put away all distractions for that time. Turn on some music and clean up.

Then, schedule at least one hour every week for cleaning your apartment again – vacuuming, cleaning your bathroom, kitchen, and bedroom... and putting things back where they belong.

Once your place looks tidy and clean, make it a habit to keep it that way every day.

Habit 19: Going after what you want

Whatever it is you want, you are missing out if you don't ask for it. Learn to say what you want openly and with confidence, start making decisions for yourself, and you will become a natural leader who will get what she wants.

Your Action Plan

Write down five things you currently want, now or in the near future. Then, for each of these, think about a way how you can ask for it or express your interest (not "show your interest subtly" – *express* it clearly!)

Make it a habit to say what you want, even if it's really hard at first. The fact is, if you make a decision or help decide something, others are often *thankful* that they don't have to decide it themselves!

Habit 20: Taking risks

Leave your comfort zone to become the amazing and successful person you want to be. Learn to see risks as necessary and good and take them whenever the potential reward is worth it. Dare to attempt even the scary things, as those usually get you the farthest (and make the best stories).

Your Action Plan

Write down at least five things you *could* do, but don't do because of the risks. Write down and rate the worst-case scenario, the realistic bad-case scenario, and the result if you succeeded, and then finally, the likelihood of each.

This should help you put things in perspective so you can dare more, take more risks, and start succeeding!

There's the saying of doing something every day that scares you. Make this mindset your habit and dare harm-less-but-frightening things when you come across them. You will outgrow your old, scared self faster than you'd believe.